*Memories of Service with the
Royal Ulster Constabulary GC 1922 to 1970*

By
JOHN NAGLE *with* **LIAM KELLY** *on behalf of the*
ROYAL ULSTER CONSTABULARY GC FOUNDATION

All rights reserved. No part of this publication may be reproduced, stored in a retrieval system or transmitted in any form or by any means, electronic, mechanical, photocopying, scanning, recording or otherwise, without the prior written permission of the copyright owners and publisher of this book.

Published by Royal Ulster Constabulary George Cross Foundation © 2010

Designed by April Sky Design, Newtownards
www.aprilsky.co.uk

Printed by GPS Colour Graphics Limited, Belfast

ISBN 978-0-9552845-2-6

LOTTERY FUNDED

Contents

	Acknowledgements 5
	Foreword 7
1	A Brief History of the Force, 1922-1969 9
2	Recruitment and Training 20
3	On the Beat: Rural Policing 30
4	Urban Policing 43
5	Social Conditions 54
6	The RUC during the Blitz 61
7	Women in the RUC 72
8	Sport in the RUC 80
9	The Customs Unit 85
10	Postscript – The 'Troubles' 91
	Notes 99
	Interviewees Cited 100
	Our Volunteer Interviewers 101

> **Dedication**
> Dedicated to those officers who did not survive to tell their stories.

Oral History Project Team and Editorial Board

Jim McDonald
(Chairman)

Murray Cameron
(Project Manager)

Freddie Hall
(Trustee RUC GC Foundation)

Hastings Donnan
(Academic Advisor, Queen's University Belfast)

John Offer
(Academic Advisor, University of Ulster)

Linda Ballard
(Academic Advisor, Ulster Folk and Transport Museum)

Acknowledgements

This book is based on, and prompted by, material gathered as part of the ongoing compilation of an Oral History of the RUC GC. Not all the material gathered has been used as the Foundation was anxious to give a view of the rich history of policing which exists but rest assured all the stories are valued and safely stored for use in the future.

The Royal Ulster Constabulary George Cross Foundation was created by virtue of the Police Act (NI) 2000 for the purposes of 'marking the sacrifices and honouring the achievements of the Royal Ulster Constabulary'. The Trustees of the Foundation, at an early stage in its life, took the view that the completion of an Oral History of the RUC GC would fit well with the Foundation's statutory purpose. The successful conclusion of a pilot scheme led to the acquisition of funding from the Heritage Lottery Fund and the project is now well established. To date over 150 interviews have been conducted with former members of the force and their families with over 120 hours of interviews being archived. The Foundation wishes to acknowledge the work of Roger Maxwell and Anthony D Buckley who were involved in the initial stages of the Project Board and Pilot Scheme.

The Foundation thanks the Heritage Lottery Fund for their generous financial support and acknowledges the work of Raymond Orr in working along with the HLF to secure the funding.

The Foundation gratefully acknowledges the work of the team of volunteer interviewers who recorded the interviews and Susan Hutton for her professionalism in transcribing the material gathered. The two full time staff of the Foundation are also due recognition for their support of all aspects of the project throughout its duration.

The Foundation acknowledges the help of Hugh Forrester and

Neil Simpson of the Police Museum for the provision of the police photographs used in the publication. Our thanks are also due to Mervyn Best, Errol Dunne, Bob Porter, Chris Ryder and Willie Brown for their helpful advice.

John Nagle and Liam Kelly would especially like to thank Jim McDonald and Hastings Donnan for their insightful comments on various drafts of this account.

CLARENCE HOUSE

As Patron of the Royal Ulster Constabulary George Cross Foundation, I am delighted to be able to contribute this foreword to the first part of a major project looking at the oral history of the Royal Ulster Constabulary.

Oral history relays the memories of service in a way in which academic history can never do and, therefore, gives accounts of history which are all the more telling for being so personal.

I look forward to the completion of the oral history project and hearing the memories of earlier times from those who gave such long and loyal service to the Constabulary.

We Remember

Chapter 1

A Brief History of the Force, 1922-1969

The Royal Ulster Constabulary (RUC) officially came into existence on 1 June 1922, one year after the establishment of the Northern Ireland Parliament. The new force took over policing duties from its predecessor the Royal Irish Constabulary (RIC). The RUC was established along the lines of the recommendations put forward by a Committee of Inquiry on police reorganisation in Northern Ireland. Chaired by Lloyd Campbell MP, the Committee proposed that the RUC should consist of a single province-wide force numbering 3,000 men, thus rejecting the County and County Borough force system which operated in Great Britain. The Committee also recommended that one-third of the Force be Catholic and that initially the majority of the RUC be recruited from the ranks of the RIC and the Specials.[1]

The RUC was a force built from the top down, with the more senior posts assigned first. For this reason it took a number of years before the RUC fulfilled its quota as laid out by the Campbell Committee.[2] By June 1923 it only had 1,100 men and it was not

Revolver training at Enniskillen under the watchful eye of the Sergeant Instructor. Note the recruits are wearing navy blue battle dress.

until 1927 that it finally hit the 3,000 mark. The Force was made up of 2,489 Constables, 300 Sergeants, 58 Head Constables, 35 District Inspectors and 6 County Inspectors. The titles were a legacy of the RIC and it was only in late 1969, with the recommendations put forward in the Hunt Report, that the RUC's rank structure was brought into line with that of other United Kingdom (UK) police forces. For an institution proud of its RIC heritage this particular reform was one of the 'more iconoclastic' in its history.[3]

By 1934, following the retirement of a number of policemen who had originally transferred from the RIC, the religious breakdown of the Force stood at 2,303 Protestants compared to 495 Catholics, from a total force of 2,798, somewhat below the recommended one-third put forward by the Campbell Committee.

Unlike other UK police forces, the RUC was charged not only with normal law enforcement tasks but also with protecting the new state of Northern Ireland and preventing armed subversion.[4] This distinction was touched upon by Sir Charles Wickham in a report he made in 1926 in response to a proposal that the RUC adopt the GB 'Village Constable' system.

> *The Ulster police is an armed force distributed in parties sufficient to provide adequate force should necessity arise, and to perform within the sub-district all the duties allotted to the police. ... A comparison of the police system of England and Ireland is not really possible because each was evolved to meet the conditions in two dissimilar circumstances.* [5]

As such – unlike police officers in Great Britain – RUC men were armed with a .45 Webley revolver and had access to rifles and bayonets, although bayonets were used only for ceremonial and parade purposes.

By the end of the 1930s the RUC had transformed itself as an effective police force with the completion of an £800,000 scheme that refurbished 196 of the original 224 RIC police stations it had inherited. Many of these buildings were antiquated and were simply modified domestic dwellings. In January 1930 a Police Traffic Branch was formed and by November 1936 a new Depot had been established in Enniskillen, replacing the original training camp at Newtownards. In May 1937 a new white glass lamp, replete with the RUC crest, went up for the first time at four stations in Belfast following criticism that many of the police buildings still displayed RIC barracks plates on them. At the close of the decade the Criminal Investigation Department (CID) had been greatly expanded and strengthened with a CID force operating in all five of Belfast's police districts.

'Sergeant and six' outside a rural station in the early 50's with the new station lamp over the front door.

In 1943 the RUC, for the first time, established a women's section under the leadership of Sergeant Marion Macmillan, who had transferred from the London Metropolitan Police. She was remembered as being

> *a really good officer. She knew what she was about and she was a very good teacher'.*

By 1944 the first six RUC policewomen had passed out of the training Depot at Enniskillen and had taken up their duties, although female police officers were initially awarded less pay than their male colleagues.

In August 1945 Sir Charles Wickham was replaced as Inspector General by the Ulster-born Richard Pim, who as a Royal Navy officer had been in charge of Winston Churchill's Map Room during World War Two. Pim was described as being 'direct, down to earth and frequently good-humoured'.[6] In the post-war period the RUC began to transform itself into a modern police unit. The Traffic Branch was significantly increased with the addition of twenty-six new cars and the assignment of a hundred extra officers. Also, a fleet of vehicles equipped with radio telephones, operating out of the Belfast Commissioner's office at Templemore Avenue, was established vastly increasing the Force's capacity to respond to 999 emergency calls. In 1950 a Reserve Force was created initially consisting of 100 men but rising to 296 by 1969. This comprised a number of mobile units specially trained for counter terrorism and public order duties. In 1957 the traditional high-necked collar for men was replaced by an open-necked tunic complete with collar and tie.

The 1950s brought its own challenges when the Force experienced its first major wave of retirements as the original batch of RUC men completed their 30 years' service. On 11 December 1956 the IRA launched its new offensive, codenamed 'Operation Harvest', with a number of coordinated attacks on police barracks throughout Northern Ireland, particularly those situated in and around the border. The so-called 'Border Campaign' claimed its first RUC casualty on 30 December 1956 when Constable John Scally was killed during an attack on the police barracks at Derrylin. By the end of the campaign, in February 1962, six RUC men had lost their lives. For many police officers their experiences of the Border Campaign would prove formative, as one officer recalled.

> *It brought a whole change to everything. Sangers were placed outside the stations at the gates, sandbags were placed in the windows, inside and outside the windows.*

Recruits at Depot Enniskillen 1955. L Squad.
Front row (left to right): Const. Ross, Sgt. Torney, Sgt. Trimble, Mr Corbett, D.I. Mr J. J. Dobbin, Commandant, Hd. Const. Irvine, Sgt. Murtagh, Sgt. McCullough, Const. Dobbin.

A early water cannon, circa 1957, with Con Albert Matchett at the controls.

... Bren guns and machineguns were in the bedrooms and under the bed, and under your pillow you had your .45 revolver.

In January 1961 Albert Kennedy, who had served as Pim's deputy, became the RUC's third Inspector General. Belfast-born Kennedy, the son of a Detective Sergeant, had worked his way up through the ranks and was renowned as being a 'copper's copper'.[7] Under Kennedy's leadership the force was to experience a number of significant changes, including the establishment of a new headquarters at Knock in 1962, and a number of rural stations were closed in the wake of advances in the RUC's mobile support capacity. In 1967 a forty-two hour week was implemented, adding to other improvements to working conditions which had previously been secured, such as the £45 wage in 1954.

Reserve Force members at Madden Rectory – Middletown/Keady Co Armagh, circa 1959.

The mid to late 1960s would prove a tumultuous period for Northern Ireland as a civil rights movement began its campaign of street politics. At this time the strength of the regular force was still pegged at immediate post-war levels of around 3,000 men and women. Starting with the October 1968 march in the city of

Londonderry, a number of significant demonstrations and counter-demonstrations began a momentous sequence of events that would change the course of Northern Ireland's and the RUC's history. By the summer of 1969 the police found themselves overstretched and working beyond their capacity. With the traumatic events of August 1969 leading to the introduction of British troops on the streets of Northern Ireland, issues surrounding policing and the general administration of law and order were never going to be the same again.

As part of a wider programme of reforms a judicial committee under the chairmanship of Lord Hunt was tasked with producing a report on policing in Northern Ireland. The result of this was the 'Advisory Committee on Policing in Northern Ireland' (October 1969), which put forward a number of major reforms for the Royal

Part of the expanded fleet of radio equipped vehicles which will be used from 146 stations outside the cities 1964.

Ulster Constabulary. These proposals recommended that the RUC 'should be relieved of all duties of a military nature as soon as possible'; the establishment of both a Police Authority and a Police Advisory Board; a review of the rank structure; the disarmament of the RUC; and the disestablishment of the Ulster Special Constabulary which was to be replaced by a 'locally recruited part-time force'.[8]

Sir Arthur Young, a former Commissioner of the City of London Police, was brought in as Inspector General and a number of English police officers were introduced to oversee these reforms. In the wake of the publication of the Hunt Report rioting broke out in the Shankill Road after loyalists protested at the nature of the recommendations. During the violence, Constable Victor Arbuckle became the first police casualty of the modern 'Troubles' on 11 October 1969. In all, 302 RUC officers were to lose their lives in the line of duty. It was in the post-1969 period that the men and women of the RUC would have to face a whole new range of challenges.

Table 1: **List of Inspectors General, 1922-1969**

- Lt. Col. Sir Charles Wickham, K.C.M.G., K.B.E., D.S.O., June 1922
- Sir Richard Pim, K.B.E., V.R.D., D.L., August 1945
- Sir Albert Kennedy, K.P.M., January 1961
- Mr. J.A. Peacock, C.B.E., February 1969
- Sir Arthur Young, C.M.G., C.P.O., K.P.M., November 1969 (Inspector General, later Chief Constable)

Table 2: **Religious breakdown of the RUC in 1934**

	Prot	R.C.	Total
Inspector General	1	–	1
Deputy I.G.	1	–	1
County Inspectors	6	3	9
District Inspectors	36	5	41
Head Constables	45	26	71
Sergeants	316	139	455
Constables	1898	322	2220
	2303	**495**	**2798**

Table 3: **RUC Police Barracks, 1922**

	RUC	RIC in 1914
Antrim	33	39
Armagh	23	27
Down	43	44
Fermanagh	23	25
Londonderry	19	22
Tyrone	33	35
City of Derry	6	5
City of Belfast	27	27
	207	**224**

Chapter 2

Recruitment and Training

I saw the police officer not only as the man who protected me but I also saw him as I grew up as somebody who could contribute something to society, to community life something positive, in the midst of all the turmoil, and I felt that was something I wanted to do. I wanted to make a difference.

∽

Very few teenagers from my part of the country went to grammar schools and I only knew two in a radius of several miles who went to university and graduated. That was my option to join the RUC as a job; I wasn't particularly drawn to it, but I had no option.

Enlistment and the Examinations

Some were practically born into it; others fell into it by chance. Some took to it like a fish to water; others felt a fish out of water, trying to make sense of the bewildering turn their lives had suddenly taken. It is impossible to ascribe a single motive to men and women deciding to enlist and serve in the RUC. Certainly, many people grew up in families that spanned generations of policemen and women.

> *My family connection with the police goes back to the RIC when my great uncle William Copithorne joined on the 15th June 1898. He was from county Cork and he would be my first known connection with the constabulary in Ireland. My father had been in the 'B' Specials prior to the war but then he was taken into the RUC.*

Even if they had no immediate family ties to the police, some felt a sense of destiny impelling them to join.

> *I do remember on one occasion coming in from school as a very young boy, and a policeman was sitting in our kitchen writing in a big book and getting details of all the animals that we had on the farm and the crops that were growing and my mother was giving him his tillage returns. I must have stood looking at this man for some time because he stooped down and lifted his police cap from the floor and he put it on my head and he said 'Son, someday you'll make a policeman'.*

Job security, regular pay and a seemingly exciting career enticed many to enlist.

> *After I attended school I went into an architects' office for a while and I worked in there, but I couldn't really see any future in it because to get anywhere in that world I required degrees and very few people were going to university in my generation so I saw that I would have to take up something else and I thought of the police and I thought of the services*

An early Passing Out Parade at the Depot Enniskillen, mid 1940s. Drill was always an important part of a constable's training.

> *and my mother told me that there are no grey hairs in the Air Force, why don't you try for the police.*

Once a person had made the momentous decision to join the police the customary next step for the prospective recruit was to make contact with their local police station where they completed an application form. A short time later the applicant was asked to come in to the station and take part in an entrance examination. The entrance examination was particularly feared by some applicants. Prior to World War Two, one man, Mr Bates in Londonderry, advertised tuition for the examination by post. After the 1948

Chapter 2: Recruitment and Training

Education Act, a recruit could gleefully avoid the examination on condition that they already held a Senior Certificate, which exempted them from the educational questions paper in any subsequent promotion examinations.

> The written test would have been English, a bit of reading a bit of literature, and then a wee maths test, which was basic sums to see if you could add and divide and subtract and things like that.

The examination could also include questions asking who were the Patron Saints of England, Scotland, Ireland and Wales. One question called upon the candidate to explain why they wanted to join the RUC, while another asked them to describe the most unusual person they had met. After they passed the test, an interview with the District Inspector and later the County Inspector followed. If the County Inspector approved the recruitment, HQ's final acceptance was a formality, subject to the medical examination. For this the recruit was asked to attend an interview at Waring Street in Belfast or Castlereagh Station, where they would also be weighed and measured for height, surely a nerve-wracking experience.

> I was called to Belfast for examination to see if I would be accepted and the conditions were rather odd. You brought all your clothes with you that you required plus the princely sum of £2. You went there and there was a Doctor Graham. You stood stark naked for examination by him, the Commandant was there and I don't know what other officers were there. From that a number of us were accepted and one or two who looked physically fit, very strong, were rejected, I think because of colour blindness for one reason.

For some recruits the experience of being weighed and measured

A barrack room ready for inspection at the Newtownards Depot, 1930s.

Recruits class in the Newtownards Depot, pre 1936.

for height was decidedly stressful, especially if they were unsure that they could make the strict specifications.

> They slipped two little pieces of paper under your heels so that you couldn't stand up on your toes and they weighed me, I was only 10 stone 10 but I was 6 feet 1 ½ inches and at home they used to call me 'tin ribs', and fair enough you could have counted the ribs down each side.

In the weeks prior to the height and weight examination, a slightly enfeebled recruit would work-out to ensure they would pass.

> In those days you had to be a minimum of 5' 9" and you had to have an average chest measurement deflated and inflated of 36 inches. I had a friend called Pat who was into the wrestling and the weightlifting and I was discussing this with him and he says 'oh no let me measure you', and I was about 33/34 round the chest – we were skinny wee boys. He says 'oh no problem I'll have that on ye, how long is it 'til you're being measured?' It was five weeks so he took me to the gym, lift weights and wrestled and do all this stuff, and when I went for me measurement I was 37 inches round the chest.

The Depot

Once the recruit had made it past the various entrance exams and interviews they were sent to receive five or six months' training at the Depot. Between 1922 and 1936 the Depot was located in Newtownards in an old army barracks. Conditions at the Depot could be described as 'primitive'.

> Now the camp at Newtownards was rough. There was this hut; it housed about twenty; eight or ten up each side. No

Following the WWI experience of gas attacks, this picture shows an anti-gas course just prior to WWII.

heat except one American style circular stove. The beds of course were coir fibre mattresses and we were given police uniforms already worn, they weren't new at that stage.

We went into the local shop and bought a fish supper and took it back, and some of the boys would leave some of the fish supper on the table and get into bed, and the next thing there would be a squealing match and the rats would be in cleaning up the chips! You got a bucket of water in the morning left at each hut, a bucket of warm water and the 13 or 14 of us shaved in that particular bucket. Then

CHAPTER 2: RECRUITMENT AND TRAINING

you washed outside in a bath with cold water and that was it.

After 1936 the Depot moved to another military barracks, this time in Enniskillen. Upon arriving at the Depot the recruits were given a last chance to back out and go home. Agreeing to stay, they then swore the Oath of Allegiance to a Justice of the Peace who attested the new constables. The next morning the recruits were put on parade and sent into the local town to visit the barbers' for a 'Depot style' short, back and sides haircut.

Life in the Depot was very Spartan. You were given a supply of butter on a weekly basis and this had to last you until you got a fresh supply the next week. It was the summertime and the temperatures were very high, and very often the butter and marg was rancid before the next issue. The bedclothes consisted of Army blankets and you didn't initially wear full police uniform – you were issued with Army battle dress,

At the Depot new recruits were arranged into squads, commonly numbering circa 13 but occasionally rising to 26 or 27 if a major recruitment drive was on. Each squad was assigned a Squad Sergeant. Due to the fact that many Squad Sergeants were former members of the Irish Guards, the training often had a strong basis in military discipline.

Life in the Depot was very much like an army camp. You were paraded every morning at 9 o'clock, you were put through foot drill and later you did foot drill and rifle drill. You were issued with a Lee Enfield Rifle and a bayonet, and the instructor that we had was an ex-Irish Guardsman, as were most of the instructors in the Depot at the time.

Recruits were also expected to receive firearms training out

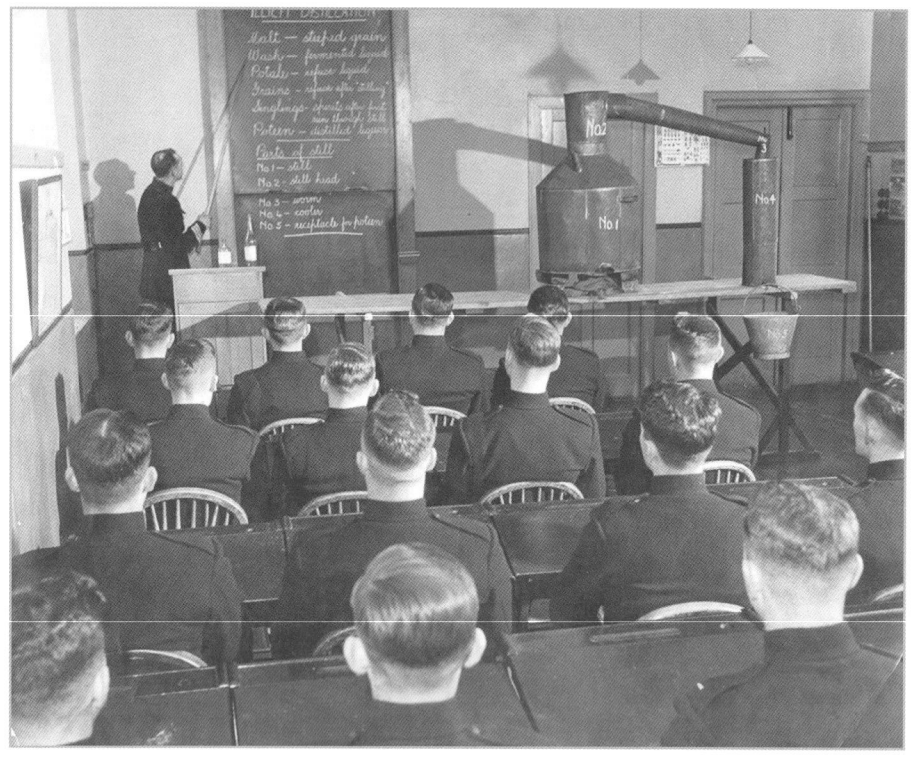

Recruits class at Depot Enniskillen. The haircuts have not changed.

on the range using an old .38 Webley service revolver. They also performed fatigues and guard duty. Alongside military drill, recruits were given strenuous physical training, including swimming in the icy pool at Portora Royal School and a five mile run. All recruits were sent to Belfast to take a driving course. Afternoons were devoted mainly to schoolwork and to first aid and there were various practical demonstrations, from traffic accidents to court proceedings. Recruits were further given written exams every month. Some of the training was not immediately appreciated by recruits but became increasingly important in later years.

One of the most important things which I learnt in the

> *Depot, although I didn't realise it at the time – I thought it was maybe a bit sissy in ways – we had to go to the tech weekly to learn typewriting. It didn't seem much sense at the time but looking back now it was probably one of the most useful things I ever learned in the police, what with the use of keyboard skills now with computers. I find now that I'm able to use that skill to a great extent and I'm glad I certainly did typewriting.*

Sunday was marked by the absence of training and in the morning recruits took part in a compulsory church parade, though by the 1960s this practice had been abandoned.

> *The compulsory church parades were interesting, in so far as there was a drill for going to church. You paraded on ground, but you did not fall in in the usual system of tallest on the right and shortest on the left in single rank size. You actually fell in by the religion and location of your church and the geography of the town meant that the Presbyterians and the Methodists fell in to the right and then the Church of Ireland and Roman Catholics fell in to their left. We came back on an informal walk on the way back as the services did not all end at the same time.*

Coming towards the end of training, there was only one last thing recruits wished to learn: to which station they would be assigned.

Chapter 3

On the Beat: Rural Policing

I was assigned to the senior man, who had 22 years' service, a man of vast experience. His first words were 'You have left the factory we will now do good police work!' Words which I have never forgotten.

⸏

I was told that I was going out to Derrylin. The Head Major said 'we're taking you out in a helicopter because there's no other way of getting out here'. That frightened me because I thought I was going into the bogs of Fermanagh, which in actual fact I was. When I met the sergeant I couldn't believe who he was. He was dressed in a pair of water boots, yellow corduroy trousers, a grandfather shirt with no collar, and the hair standing on his head. When he came to the door I opened it and asked him, who he was. He says 'I'm your sergeant!' He then asked me to turn on the lights as it was getting dark. It was a winter night, and

CHAPTER 3: ON THE BEAT: RURAL POLICING

being a townie I looked round for a light switch and I saw one in the hall and I turned it on. All the alarm bells in the station rang, apparently these were worked on batteries and he grabbed me by the arm and said 'Look, son, you're not in the Depot now, we have no lights, no electric lights here...'

Recruits had no power to choose the station to which they were allocated. It was standard practice to post new recruits to rural stations and not to Belfast unless there were compelling personal reasons for doing so. However, recruits who excelled at sports, or who were destined for the RUC Band, were immediately posted to a station in Belfast. Most rural stations were small and staffed by one Sergeant and between four to six men. In times of unrest, the Ulster

A brisk walk along the seafront in Bangor.

31

Special Constabulary supplemented the numbers.

If conditions at the Depot appeared basic to recruits, many were in for an almighty surprise when they first reported for duty at the station to complete their two years' probationary training. Men and women who had grown up in towns and cities would often be assigned to remote rural stations and they could have scarcely predicted prior to arrival how backward life was in the station. The shock was as palpable as the homesickness.

> *There were three beds in this wee darkened room with one light bulb in it. I remember half one in the morning looking out pitch black, one wee light, and wondering what on earth I had done? What had I done? I had left Belfast where there was electricity there was cars, there was bustle, hustle everything, there was nothing here!*

Rather than the exception, it was common for rural stations to have no running water, gas or electricity. These rural barracks were inherited from the RIC and many were in bad shape after undergoing attacks from the IRA. Unsurprisingly, new recruits viewed conditions at the station as 'primitive'.

> *The only heating in the whole place was the coal fire in the Enquiry Office. There was no such thing as power sockets for electric fires. There was no such thing as drinking water in the station. The pipe water was sucked from the River Bann, which was about 20 metres away and there were no mechanical pumps to fill the cistern in the station. It was just a hand pump. I think it was called a 'Cows Tail Handle Pump'. It didn't work very well either, there was a leak from the valves and whether it was raining or not you were still going to get splashed, so you had to wear your bicycle cape when you were pumping. It was the duty*

CHAPTER 3: On the Beat: Rural Policing

of the Station Orderly, who had finished duty at 9 am, having been on duty in the Enquiry Room for 24 hours; and it was his duty to start pumping the water with the Cows Tail at 10 o'clock until he had filled the tank. The river water wasn't filtered or sterilised in any way and the only thing you could use it for was for washing the floor. In fact I had seen dead cattle and dogs partially submerged, leaving nearby Lough Neagh and passing our inlet pipe.

Once the new recruits had adjusted to the conditions at the country station, life in the 'slow lane' could be highly amenable, if slightly eccentric.

The station was quite handy because it was just on the verge of Lough Melvin. On a nice summer day you just went out and swam in Lough Melvin and the sergeant's wife raised the flag if you were wanted in.

Officers who had acquired a trade before enlisting with the police often engaged in extra-curricular activities in the local village.

The local butcher who usually came along on market day and he knew I was a butcher and asked me if I would mind helping his daughter out in serving up the meat. So there I am in full police uniform, revolver, the lot and serving the beef.

The common mode of transport for the rural police was the trusted bicycle and cycle patrol would last 3½ hours. There were two of these each day and were varied over the 24 hours. For those whose bike patrol took them close to the Irish border, it was often difficult to determine where the border began and ended.

I was out on my own, on one of the border roads, which in those days weren't even tarred, the roads leading towards

33

An unarmed constable in Downpatrick.

the border were known as sand and dirt roads, and, I must have missed where the border actually was, because I had cycled on quite a bit and then stopped where this man, who was quite friendly and chatted to me for a wee while, and he said, 'do you know what I'm going to tell you? It's thirty years since I seen one of your men down here.' And I said, 'Why, what's wrong?' 'Well,' he says, 'you're just about a mile on the Free State side of the border.'

There was a report of an accident. Donald went out on his bicycle, down the main road, and a motorcycle and his pillion passenger had come to grief on a bad corner. And it was obvious to me that the pillion passenger was dead. This was my first fatal accident. There was no back-up. I had a tape in my hand, that was all. There was no telephone communication, you didn't have it, it was the day before pocket phones. There was nothing. But I… Somebody had told, sent for an ambulance. And with the help of what motorists was there, and people that stopped, you encouraged them to help you, the ambulance came and we got the driver away, and the dead body away. And I tidied, did what I could, and tidied up the scene. And I was quite worried, because this was my first fatal accident. I knew I had a coroner's report to do, and of course the investigation of the accident. [pause] And gathering up the bits and pieces, what did I come on in the middle of this, but a shoe and part of a leg, on the remains of the bicycle. So, I think … There was no fancy bags in those days, forensic bags, there was nothing. Somehow or other, I think, a motorist gave me a, a piece of newspaper, and I got it round, and I tied it onto the back of my bicycle, and I cycled off to the Lagan Valley Hospital to pursue my enquiries. [pause] Now, I went into the office, the reception area, and my whole worry was, what was I going to do with the leg? How would I get all the details for the immediate report of this serious accident, and get enough details for the coroner? And there was a dead body to be examined, and a leg to be disposed of.

I think it was a Tuesday I was on Town Duty … John McDonagh was coming through the town on Greencastle Street on a flat open cart. He was sitting at the front and his wife was sat on the tail end, and they had an old bicycle on the cart and him and her had some words and he threw the bicycle off the cart, hitting the headlamp of a car that was parked. But he just put the bicycle on the cart and drove on. I was eventually found and told about what had happened and where this man had gone on his pony and cart. I enquired first from the garage across the way what it would cost to repair and was told £3.7.6 old money. I got my bicycle and I cycled out to the Newcastle Road. I questioned him about paying up for the damage to this car but he had no money, he assured me he had no money and the wife had no money and the only thing of value I thought was the old bicycle and I didn't think it was worth £3. And then I spotted the piebald pony and I thought well it's worth a pound or two. So I untied the pony, took it in one hand and the bicycle in the other and marched them to Kilkeel. I brought the pony up and put it in the backyard and closed the gate. I felt sure he would turn up for this pony, because he couldn't travel without it. About two or three hours later he did turn up and with a lot of effort he managed to scrape up £3.7.6 and before I let him take the pony out of the yard, I made him clean up the mess the pony had made.

For those stationed on a river or lough, transportation was augmented by a patrol boat and outboard engine.

Much of the work carried out was not directly related to crime and had more to do with administrative work regarding farming.

CHAPTER 3: ON THE BEAT: RURAL POLICING

A Constable Calls
by Seamus Heaney

His bicycle stood at the window-sill,
The rubber cowl of a mud-splasher
Skirting the front mudguard,
Its fat black handlegrips

Heating in sunlight, the "spud"
Of the dynamo gleaming and cocked back,
The pedal treads hanging relieved
Of the boot of the law.

His cap was upside down
On the floor, next to this chair.
The line if its pressure ran like a bevel
In his slightly sweating hair.

He had unstrapped
The heavy ledger, and my father
Was making tillage returns
In acres, roods, and perches.

Arithmetic and fear.
I sat staring at the polished holster
With its buttoned flap, the braid cord
Looped into the revolver butt.

" Any other root crops?
Mangolds? Marrowstems? Anything like that?"
"No." But was there not a line
Of turnips where the seed ran out

37

We Remember

In the potato field? I assumed
Small guilts and sat
Imagining the black hole in the barracks.
He stood up, shifted the baton-case

Further round on his belt,
Closed the doomsday book,
Fitted his cap back with two hands,
And looked at me as he said goodbye.

A shadow bobbed in the window.
He was snapping the carrier spring
Over the ledger. His boot pushed off
And the bicycle ticked, ticked, ticked.

Reproduced by permission of Faber&Faber.

This sergeant on patrol in Co. Fermanagh in the 1950s is riding the Police Model bike referred to in the Seamus Heaney poem 'A Constable Calls'

CHAPTER 3: On the Beat: Rural Policing

Tillage duty on Rathlin Island.

> *Well life was quiet there, and there was very little crime. But we had a number of duties to carry out for the Ministry of Agriculture. The main one of these was the tillage, which was a survey of the farms and livestock and crops of the countryside. This really originated from the famine years in the 1840s, when the crops failed, and after that the RIC, as they were at that day, had to make reports every year about May on what their crops prospects seemed to be, whether the crops would be favourable or not. This continued on until, into RUC times, then the Ministry of Agriculture expanded the whole thing and we found that we had to fill in a large book with details of everything, whether it be hens, acreage of the farm or the holding, what crops there were, what the yields were, return of livestock, and so on.*

Another thing was foxes, the Ministry paid a bounty for foxes. I think it was 10 shillings for an adult fox and 5 shillings for a cub. The instructions were that the dead animals were to be brought to the Police Station and the tongue of the animal was to be cut out and the policeman filling in the form was to see that this was done. Presumably this was to prevent somebody taking the foxes round to another Station, saying it had been shot somewhere else.

I had no experience of the country. I was a townie. I had lived all my life in Belfast. Here was a new, completely new experience for me. It was a social job. There was really nothing to do as a police officer. You engaged with the community, you talked to them, you tried to get tea in their houses, and you looked to see if there were any eligible young girls about.

While appearances might suggest that rural policing was slow, arcane and relatively benign, it could be highly dangerous. A major source of peril emanated from the IRA's Border Campaign (1956-62). In the 1950s the IRA had begun to rearm, assisted by a number of successful attacks on British army barracks where they escaped with hauls of rifles, sub-machine and Bren guns. Intending to 'liberate' swathes of territory inside Northern Ireland, Irish republicans targeted and attacked isolated RUC barracks along the border. Even before the Border Campaign began in earnest in 1956, a break-away faction of the IRA, called Saor Uladh (Free Ulster), was causing mayhem.

At twenty minutes to six in the morning on the 26th November 1955 there was an armed attack on the police station. Now I was guard and at that time you could do the 24-hour guard, and I was in my bed in a small camp bed, revolver beside the table and of course a tilly lamp. There was a charge put in below the air vent that blew me out of bed and the police station. I was blown from the side window over to where two pillars were… and the only thing I felt was as if somebody had hit me a slap on the back. And I remember shouting 'Mummy, mummy the gas meter's just blown up!' There was no gas or electricity in Rosslea. The raiders came in through the hole in the wall, walked over the rubble. I could hear shooting in the hallway. I could see flashes coming from a gun and I could hear bullets ricocheting above my head. It seemed quite a while and the raiders came out. One shone a torch in my face, and said 'Oh! Come on he's had it" and it was just by the help of God that I kept quiet.. Eventually Charlie, who was one of the members of the station, came down and he heard me moaning and he said 'Oh lie there, you'll be alright'. Mrs Morrow came down and gave me a cup of tea. They got the wee postmaster and a Ford Thames van. I was lifted on my own mattress in my own blankets and by that time the District Inspector had arrived and told me to hold on. I was being transported to Fermanagh County Hospital. So I arrived in Fermanagh County Hospital and I was being carried into the ward and the first thing I shouted was 'No Surrender!' At that time I didn't realise how badly I was injured, but when they put me in the bed there was two hankies sticking out of my chest because I had a habit of putting two hankies into my pyjama jacket. The bullet was carried in through two inches below the heart and carried the two hankies into the chest. When *they took the 2 hankies out the bullet dropped onto the bed. I had a bullet wound through the left arm, I had one right through the left knee, I had one went in behind the knee and lodged in the ball of the leg. I had one that went into the thigh and that was a bit of shrapnel. I had one that went in through the left side. I still had three bits of shrapnel in my back and the one that I felt was one that went in through the left side, round the back of the spine and lodged one inch on the right hand side of the back. I received a first class record and £10.00 and they gave me a little plaque about the raids in Rosslea. But medals aren't everything; I've got my life, which is more important.*

Chapter 4

Urban Policing

Well, I came to Musgrave Street with very mixed feelings because in the country nobody wanted to go to Belfast, they didn't like the hours of duty and the authorities were supposed to be very tight and it wasn't a nice place to look on for a policeman. The country men didn't like to go to Belfast.

∽

When I came out of the Depot I was sent to Tennent Street in Belfast. I slept in a room above the guard room and there were two other constables in that room with me. One of them was a fellow from Fermanagh. He had a photograph of King Billy astride his white horse. And he says to me, 'Does that photograph offend you?' Says I, 'No, if it doesn't s****t e on me'. And then he says, 'I'm going to give you a bit of advice. Just because you wear an RUC uniform, you could still get a beating up the Shankill.'

An alert duo on patrol in Belfast mid 1960s.

As much as the townies initially felt disoriented trying to get to grips with the slow rhythms of country policing, the sons of the farm also experienced culture shock when they were assigned to the town or the city after training.

> *I arrived on the Lisburn Road and remember well standing in the road looking up and down and watching all these*

big trams and all this traffic going up and down and it was a big, big move from the quiet streets of Kilrea I can tell you.

Before the major increase in car numbers the flow of traffic particularly at peak periods was the responsibility of the police.

Harry White did the Point. Harry was famous. He did the Point up in Shaftesbury Square. I mean some of the things that happened there are unbelievable. I can remember the summertime the barman used to waltz out of Mosey Hunter's with a tray and the pint on the top of it across the crossing to Harry and Harry was standing in the middle of the crossing drinking his pint of beer and put it back on the tray and the boy would take it back to Mosey Hunter's pub.

I'll tell you a funny story about Harry. There come down one day an old green Zephyr you see and Harry had all the traffic stopped. He looked in and this boy was wearing a green Army sweater. Harry said to him 'Are you a soldier?' The boy says, 'Yeah, yeah, I am.' He says, 'Do you know the Quartermaster Sergeant well?' 'Yeah', he says, I know him fairly well'. He says, 'What's the possibility of getting a pair of Army boots for I'm standing in this crossing day in and day out?' He says, 'And the only thing that would keep my feet right are these Army boots'. And the guy in the car says, 'leave it with me'. So about a month later Harry's doing the Point and up comes an official green car, pennants flying from the front of it, two MPs, one driving, one sitting in the front, bodyguard. There's the GOC in the back and he waves Harry over and the window goes down and he hands Harry this parcel. He says, 'the

We Remember

With the increase in traffic, the points man was essential to keep the traffic flowing. Circa 1965, Belfast.

Quartermaster Sergeant sent you that'. The window goes up and the car drives off and Harry's standing there with this parcel. So back over to the station, opens the parcel and there were six sets of Army boots, all size nine, for Harry.

... there was Point Duty. That was at the junction above the Royal Victoria Hospital in Belfast and the Springfield Road and the Falls Road area, and often I did Point Duty there at that particular place. And sometimes we had tram drivers when they came along and you stopped them, if there was a supervision sergeant in the area, they put their fingers over on their left arm to let you know that there was a sergeant in the area, or if it was a head constable they had observed, they put their fingers to their head to let you know there was a head constable was on supervision.

Living quarters for the police stationed in the city could be every bit as rough as in the rural barracks.

A constable from Musgrave Street on the point at Laganbank Road.

> *I was sent to Belfast to York Street, which was a terrible old house, whitewashed walls, bedrooms old brown lino and old iron bed, and it was up in the attic. The accommodation was terrible: you made your own breakfast in the morning, a lady came in and made the dinner, you went off duty in the afternoon made your own tea and you had to be in for 11 pm each night. Then on one occasion in the winter months it was snowing badly and I was lying in bed, and the water came through the roof onto my bed. I was taken to hospital and spent three weeks in hospital with the pleurisy because of the conditions.*

On the beat in Belfast city centre was particularly prized as it was here that the police were highly noticeable. The fact that there was a minimum height restriction for police patrolling the city centre emphasized the almost out-of-the-ordinary appearance of the officers.

> *When I arrived there I met a guy in the guard room and he said to me 'I'm glad to see you', and I said 'Why?' He says 'Now you're the smallest man in the station'. He says 'I'm 6' 1½" and I'm small.' The average height was about 6' 3" and in those days you had to be well over 6' to get into the city centre. I remember going out on night duty with the night helmet on and there were guys 6'6". There was the sergeant, Jimmy, he was 6' 8".*

Once the officer became accustomed to policing in Belfast, they could gradually avail of all the activities typical of big city life.

CHAPTER 4: URBAN POLICING

Well after I was in it a week I realised to myself that I had landed on my feet, that I had all day until 5 o'clock in the evening when I had to parade for evening duty. I could go where I liked, there were picture houses, there were dance halls, cafés, restaurants, shops of all sorts, there was the Empire and I still had my motorbike and 15 minutes would take me down to the seaside. Life was great!

Despite the obvious attractiveness of immediate cultural pleasures, policing in the city was hazardous and dangerous for a number of reasons.

It was teatime, it was rush hour traffic and I was on beat duty up at the Ardoyne and one well-known hood from Chatham Street appeared at McCann's fish and chip shop and he was in a rather drunken state. He started to

'Urban or rural the bike was the popular mode of transport and the bicycle allowance augmented the income.'

Mobile patrol in Belfast stretch their legs.

carry on in the chip shop and was causing a bit of bother and the lady who was behind the counter came out and called at me to come down and get him out, because he was being disorderly. I went down and remonstrated with the gentleman and got him out onto the footpath. I was just opposite the fire station when suddenly I got hit from behind. I don't know what it was that hit me, hit from behind and I suddenly realised that I was under a physical attack. Rolled myself into a ball, rolled across the footpath and stood up and discovered that the gentleman that I had ushered off the premises five minutes beforehand had come back, armed with a post of some description and he set about me with this post and the two of us had a right old ding dong on the footpath. We ended up in the middle of the road, with double decker buses screeching brakes, horns blowing, at this policeman with a raincoat and a cap that no longer was on his head wrestling with this fellow with a big lump of wood.*

Occasionally, Constables could be their own worst enemies.

At 11 p.m. on the 11th of July Constable Barney finished his evening duty at Cullingtree Road Barracks and prepared to make his way home to his lodgings on Lisburn Road by pedal cycle, a journey he would have done hundreds of times. His usual and direct route was Roden Street, Donegall Avenue, Tate's Avenue Bridge. At the bridge, he would carry his bicycle up the steps and remount on Tate's Avenue, finally emerging on to Lisburn Road. However, on 11th of July 1951 things did not go entirely to plan. The Constable enjoyed a liberal amount of liquid refreshment on his beat between 6 p.m. and 11 p.m.; accordingly, when he began to cycle home he was well under the weather. In his inebriated state he made a right turn off Donegall Avenue, Road [...] and according to witnesses rode straight into the bonfire at Broadway Parade, like a moth to a candle. He went head-over-heels into the fire, and only the prompt action of onlookers preserved him from serious injury. When the back-up crew arrived he had been taken into a nearby house, having his face and hands bathed in cold water. His uniform cap had been completely consumed in the flames and his long waterproof coat was partly burnt and melted. The front wheel of his bicycle was buckled and part of the tyre burnt. On ascertaining that the constable was not seriously injured, the crew drove him to his home, before returning to me at Roden Street.

Although Belfast was immune from the IRA's Border Campaign, chronic bouts of rioting occurred in the city during the mid-1960s. On one infamous occasion in 1964 an Irish Nationalist flag was placed in the window of an Irish Republican office in Divis Street area of Nationalist west Belfast. The Loyalist leader, Ian Paisley, threatened to lead a mob to remove the flag if the police did not intervene. In front of a large crowd of angry Nationalists, the police removed the flag and as a result severe riots wracked parts of Belfast for days.[9]

> *I arrived in Belfast in 1964 and was put on night duty. And that was very interesting, because there were the riots, the first riots that I had experienced, in Divis Street. The flag that was in the office there was a Starry Plough, which many people did not know the significance of, but Paisley objected to it, and the police had to go, and I remember it, and I know the sergeant who took it out of the window, broke the window and took it out, the Starry Plough. Well there were riots then, immediately after that. And I had been on night duty, was drafted over to it. The local population had been disturbed, and reacted, and the police reacted against them. Not a pleasant scene.*

Even before the outbreak of the 'Troubles' in 1969, underlying tensions in the city meant that policing was fraught with anxiety.

> *I moved to Belfast to Springfield Road and then I met an auld fella and he says 'George, you'll not be initiated into this Station until you get a hand grenade thrown at you.'*

Despite the ever-present dangers associated with the job, the cohesive glue of comradeship and a rich social life ensured that life in the Force could be highly rewarding.

Pay and Conditions of Service

Although in the early years pay did not seem to be a driver in encouraging recruitment, the fact that it was a continuous job with regular pay and a pension was no doubt an attraction when even in the industrialised cities very few men had uninterrupted employment for a whole year at a time.

Entrance Requirements

Chest: At least 36"
Height: Minimum 5'10"
Marriage: Candidates under 21 must be single

Constables' Pay

	1947		**1969**
On joining	£273 p.a.	Aged 18	£765 p.a.
2-9 years' service	£281-£334 p.a.	Aged 19	£765 p.a.
10-16 years' service	£343 p.a.	Aged 20	£800 p.a.
17-21 years' service	£359 p.a.	Aged 21	£835 p.a.
22 years upwards	£364 p.a.	Aged 22	£870 p.a.

Rising to a maximum of £1205

Women Constables' Pay

Aged 20   £720
Aged 21   £750
Aged 22   £785

Allowances

Rent Allowance: £7.72 p.a.
Boot Allowance: £5.20 p.a.

Chapter 5

Social Conditions

At this stage of my life I came alive. I was tremendously proud of becoming a full-time member of the RUC and to wear its uniform ... These were the years when the police were respected and looked upon as having a certain standing in the community. As a young constable of twenty three years of age, it gave me a great sense of importance and at last I'd gathered myself up and out of the gutters through my own determination and the longing to improve my quality of life.

Socialising

For the men and women of the RUC the pattern of their social life largely depended on where they were stationed. The fact that members of the force were not allowed to serve in areas where their family members lived limited the amount of time they could spend back home on leave.

Going to Newry was a culture shock for me. It was

CHAPTER 5: SOCIAL CONDITIONS

three miles from home. I had to take the bus from Newry to Belfast, and then the train from Belfast to Londonderry where I lived, and then a bus home. It really took a whole day when you coordinated the timetables.

All 'time off', especially 'private business', was strictly monitored and tightly controlled.

But leave was of course a privilege, not a right, and the first requirement was the exigencies of the service. In other words, if there wasn't enough men to do the recognised beats or other duties that were being called on, like court duty or something like that, then the sergeant would shake his head and say, 'Sorry, can't let you away on leave that day, because we need you, we haven't enough men'. And that was that.

But during the time you were off, you had to stay in the barracks. You were allowed out two hours' private business during the day, and you were allowed one weekend off a month, and you had fourteen days' annual leave, which you had to apply for. Now, if you wished to take a weekend, you had to apply for it, and you had to apply for private business. It was very, very draconian, and very much back in the Middle Ages, and that was in 1965, '66.

Despite this, a well-organised approach to leave allocations could allow some officers to enjoy a substantial break away in the sun, as one former member recalls.

The funny thing about it was in 1968 there was a crowd of us from Donegall Pass went to Spain for 5 weeks and in those days you got 37 days leave plus if the Inspector

55

Even in 1964 Road Safety was a high priority for policing.

> *General thought you had done a good job, he used to give the Force a couple of days extra every year.*

A sympathetic landlady could provide cover when trying to make the most of one's off-duty time.

> *If we weren't on duty we had to be in our digs no later than eleven o'clock at night. And if we weren't on duty and had to go out shopping, we weren't to be out of our digs more than two and a half hours in any given time. We had a very understanding landlady, she would actually say, 'oh the girl had just gone out'.*

Marriage

Marriage could be a tricky affair for officers. Serving officers not only had to find a suitable spouse and convince them of the joys of betrothal, they also had to seek permission, or give a 'Notice of Intention', to the RUC hierarchy before they were allowed up the aisle.

> Well I had to give my authorities Notice of Intention of getting married. In earlier years you had to apply for permission, but in my time it was Notice of Intention. As regards the marriage itself, I was fortunate because it was the daughter of a policeman, and she knew what she was getting into, she knew that her husband would be away for all sorts of hours, at different times and so on; she knew that the police would have had first claim on him, on the husband's attendance and she would have to live with that. Well I'm glad to say I had no problems in that, my wife fully accepted me and was a great support to me I have to say.

> We also learnt about applying for permission to get married. A list of future wives' relatives down to first cousins had to be supplied. If one married without the permission of the Inspector General, that member may be required to resign. A woman member of the force had to resign on marriage.

Regulations concerning marriage were especially strictly adhered to for female officers. Like their counterparts in the civil service, once they were married they could no longer carry on with their chosen profession. It was not until 1969 that this regulation was dropped, allowing a number of former policewomen to come out of retirement and rejoin the ranks of the RUC.

> I enjoyed my time in the women police. I think I'd have made a better policewoman if I'd been able to serve longer.

The problem was, when so many of us got engaged, and then were getting married, we had to terminate our service with the RUC.

It was often during their time on duty that members of the force first met their future spouse, despite infringing upon the strict letter of the law.

So on this particular occasion I was on night duty in Andersonstown, and, as it happened, in those days, if a person committed or attempted to commit suicide, it was rated a crime. So, on this particular night there happened to be two suicides, one in the City Hospital, and one in the Royal Victoria Hospital. I was given the task of going and sitting with the patient in the City Hospital. And I duly went down and spent the night in the hospital and was catered for by some very nice, helpful nurses who gave me a meal during the night and one of those particular nurses I got friendly with and was presumptuous enough to invite her out. That young lady eventually became my wife.

One day I was doing a road block, stopping cars coming in from Newtownards and there I stopped a car which, well in fact it didn't stop. I waved my torch at it with my red lens and the car sped on. So I got on my motor-bicycle and I overtook the car and got it stopped. And it turned out that it was an elderly gentleman, a very nice man, and I said, 'Excuse me, sir, you didn't stop for my signal'. And this young woman sitting beside him decided to give me a dressing-down, saying, 'You didn't signal, you waved us on'. And that was the girl that I married later on.

Esprit de corps

It is clear, then, that membership within the ranks of the RUC helped foster a strong *esprit de corps*. Many former officers recalled the job as being highly sociable and enjoyable.

> *There were twenty-six of us in the batch of raw recruits which arrived that day. These boys all came from various parts of Northern Ireland, twenty-six young men, Catholics and Protestants together, from various backgrounds and walks of life, and yet drawn together in one purpose, to serve Queen and Country, to assist and protect the peoples of our land, and this common bond which quickly dispelled the apprehensions that separate strangers, and soon we were chatting and laughing together. It was our first experience of the comradeship that lay ahead.*

The squads bonded together and even today there are reunions, although the original members are often reduced.

40th Reunion - W Squad
12th May 1969-2009

At
Newforge Country Club

Sid

For those stationed in rural areas, the local dances were always a big attraction for the young constables. It did not matter whether the dance was held in the local Orange Hall or the parochial hall, the police were always welcome. We have stories from constables attending in uniform being given tea in the hall's kitchen, hanging the belt with baton and revolver behind the kitchen door and then advancing into the hall to survey the talent and dancing.

For those stationed in the west of the city of Belfast, it was usual for the men on the beat to drop into Clonard Monastery or Ardoyne to attend Mass on Sunday. Such was the integration of the police with the local population.

Chapter 6

The RUC during the Blitz

At the outbreak of World War Two few in the Northern Ireland government at Stormont seemed willing to countenance the fact that Belfast might be heavily bombed by the Luftwaffe. Yet Belfast, as one of the largest industrial cities in the United Kingdom, was to become a very obvious target for the Germans. One of the rare precautionary measures implemented by the government was transferring 100 police officers to Galwally House on the Ormeau Road in Belfast. 'The reason for this', one officer recalled, 'was in case Belfast was bombed there would have to be a unit of police put in the area to prevent looting'. Other than this, Belfast was dangerously under-prepared for a sustained aerial bombardment. The government thought it wasteful to spend money on civil defences and cancelled orders for fire-fighting equipment.

> *The city had no fighter squadrons, no balloon barrage and only twenty anti-aircraft guns when the war began. There were only four public air-raid shelters, made of sandbags, located at the City Hall, together with underground toilets*

Photograph taken by a "Telegraph" photographer during the height of the raid. *Belfast Telegraph*

> *at Shaftesbury Square and Donegal Square North. Not a single shelter was provided anywhere else in Northern Ireland* [10]

The first ominous portent of Belfast's bombing came in late November 1940.

> *None of us knew at that particular time that in 1940 a German airplane was seen over Belfast and was taking photographs of the targets for bombing.*

The German airplane was conducting a reconnaissance of the city and had collected detailed photographs on a number of important targets, like the shipyards, the Waterworks and Victoria Barracks. Despite the sign that an attack was imminent, little was done to defend the city or protect its vulnerable inhabitants.

> *At that particular time the authorities in the city were intending to evacuate 70,000 children out to the country, and the first lot of 17,000 were named to go, but only 7,000 turned up and half of them came back by the spring of 1941.*

The first major aerial assault came on 7 April 1941. Six Heinkel He 111s dropped high explosives, incendiary bombs and parachute mines on Belfast killing twelve people. An officer remembered the night's events.

> *At eleven o'clock we headed for home, to the police station, and all of a sudden the sky lit up, and it was bright as daylight, flares. And the next thing, we heard a whistle followed by an explosion. We knew the bombing of the city had taken place. We hurried down to the police station and got into uniform. Everybody was in the billiard room. So after a while we decided about two o'clock that it wasn't a terribly safe place to be with the bombing, we went outside and we got involved in putting out phosphorous bombs with sandbags and put out a fire in a jeweller's shop. And we spent our night and came back to the police station. Got up the next morning, only to find that there was very little damage in the city centre. Now, the following morning – the following evening, about 100,000 people left the city, by lorry and any transport they had, and made for the hills outside the city.*

This was to be a mere prelude to what was to come. Lord Haw Haw, the Nazi propaganda broadcaster, menacingly warned that there would be 'Easter eggs for Belfast'. Sure enough, on Easter Tuesday, 15 April 1941, more than 180 German bombers made their way up the Irish Sea towards Belfast. On arrival, the Luftwaffe squadrons deposited 203 metric tons of bombs and 800 fire bomb canisters on the city. North Belfast was particularly badly hit, especially the residential areas of the New Lodge, Lower Shankill, Ardoyne and Tigers Bay. The York Street Mill collapsed flattening 42 houses in the process and a large shelter on Percy Street was destroyed killing thirty people. Within three hours the telephone service was smashed. The *Belfast Newsletter* observed afterwards.

> *The wantonness and ruthlessness of the attack was appalling. Working class and residential areas suffered most. Numbers of houses have been laid waste, banks, churches, a charitable institution, industrial builders and cinemas and schools were wrecked, and at one point trees bordering an avenue were uprooted and stripped of their branches by the force of the detonations* [11]

The police were overstretched trying to rescue survivors and dampen the hundreds of fires lit by the incendiary bombs.

> *Now, on the night of April 15th, the German bombers returned, and this time they bombed the city indiscriminately. Anything was a target, particularly all around Musgrave Street, Victoria Street, High Street, Bridge Street – all demolished – even the City Hall got bombed. We went out to see and all the tramlines were down, it was a very dangerous place. We tried to work a little fire pump, but it was useless, no water. There were no fire brigades to be seen on that occasion. I can tell you right now that there was 1,000 people killed that night and 100,000 left homeless. The bodies were placed in Peter's*

The Municipal tram service carried on despite handicaps imposed by Hitler's bombs, which fell both inside and outside this depot in Salisbury Avenue (Antrim Road). *Courtesy Belfast Telegraph*

Hill, the swimming pool and the Falls Baths and the markets.

You know when I think back on it there was some very sad things because I remember after one of the big air raids that demolished all of York Road there was a woman came to me and she says 'there's a man there ... there's an unexploded bomb up the road and he's going up there and we're going to have to stop him'. So I had to run after him and there he was just walking over the road sobbing and he said 'there were ten of us in the house and there's only one of us, I'm the only one left'.

Nowhere in Belfast seemed safe that night. It was only the quick thinking of one officer that averted a disaster at York Street Barracks when he spotted a parachute mine heading straight for the station.

There was a certain Head Constable at the Barracks, no names, it was bad. He directed the men to stay inside, but Donald Flack didn't listen to him. 'Get out quick!' he said; 'there's something coming down here in a parachute'. They got out or they would all have been killed and it was Donald Flack who told them to get out!

If the police at York Street survived due to the initiative shown by Constable Flack, when the Luftwaffe returned to Belfast in early May there was little that could be done to stop tragedy striking a station on Glenravel Street, which was completely destroyed in the attack.

I don't know how many were in Glenravel Street but they were all assembled in one room and there was a sergeant and he went to the DI and said 'it was risky to have so many there in case anything happened', so they moved most of them out to air raid shelters ... but the station took a direct hit and I think reinforced walls came down on them and killed the five. It was very sad, I knew them all and I had snaps with them, you know.

Londonderry was also bombed during the 'Blitz' with 15 killed.

> There was bombs dropped in Derry City down at Shantallow there, there were cottages destroyed there.

Due to its geographic position, Derry was also a key port during the Battle of the Atlantic. It was here that shipwrecked members of the merchant navy were often taken for some brief respite after being rescued:

> It was very sad during the Battle of the Atlantic, to see the number of men coming in up Townhall Street up to what was known as the Sailors' Rest in Sackville Street. Some of them didn't have very much on them. Rescued from sea, brought in up to Sailors' Rest where they would rest, get equipped and back into the pool again to get back in again.

One officer also vividly remembers German submarines coming to Londonderry to surrender at the conclusion of the war.

> We went down to Culmore Point to see the German submarines coming into surrender, that was unusual. The crews were lined up on the top of the subs and the peculiar thing, they were nearly all streamlined the subs, we hadn't expected that. There was one sub that was brought up to behind the Guildhall and I took my father-in-law down there and we went into that submarine. My goodness, it was very claustrophobic I thought. There was a snorkel device on it for breathing, so they never needed to surface for so many days, but the periscope was tremendous. Along the harbour and the little railway line there, you could pick out anything lying on the railway line. The opticals were very good.

'The Yanks'

Outside of Belfast, one of the main changes noted by the people of Northern Ireland was the arrival of thousands of US troops. Even before the Japanese attack on Pearl Harbor, the United States War Department had formulated Rainbow 5, a plan to send over 50,000 men to England and over 20,000 men and 100 aircraft to Northern Ireland in the event of the US being dragged into the war. In January 1942 the 133rd Infantry Regiment of the 34th Infantry Division was the first United States Army unit sent to Europe in World War Two. Many of the 'yanks' were stationed near the border, where they prepared for the invasion of occupied Europe.

> *Now at the same time there was, there was anything up to 20,000 or 30,000 American soldiers all along the coast, from Kilkeel to Warrenpoint, in various places, and were there to be trained for the landing at Normandy. And they came in, their place of release, where they came to enjoy themselves, was Warrenpoint. So, we had a very good time with them, they were very good to the police. They used to bring us food, steaks and, and that sort of thing. It was tremendous, they were lovely men.*

Local Hostilities

The Germans provided a new foreign army for the police to deal with, while at home the IRA increased operations during the war with their Northern Campaign. On one occasion the IRA raided a camp in Ballykinler.

> *In the old days in the station the rifles were in a rifle rack and there was a chain which ran through them to keep them; but the night that the IRA raided Ballykinler – somebody forgot to lock the chain and the IRA got away with 30 rifles.*

Some of the guns were recovered by the police.

> *We got information that there were 5 rifles at a farm so we arrived early about midnight or so and we started to search for these 5 rifles. The dawn broke and there was no sign of them. We turned the whole place upside down. But we had an old senior man with us who was a bit of a gardener, interested in gardening and he walked right into the garden, beside the farm house and was looking up at the apple trees and there was the 5 rifles lashed to the branches of the apple trees.*

Perhaps the most infamous IRA attack during the war occurred during Easter 1942 when the IRA shot dead an officer, Patrick Murphy, in west Belfast. Tom Williams, a 17-year old IRA volunteer, was hanged in the Crumlin Road Gaol for his involvement in the killing. The son of the murdered officer recounted the killing.

> *On the 5th of April 1942, Easter Sunday, my father and three colleagues were travelling in a police car along Clonard Street. While passing an air raid shelter shots were fired at the car by six IRA men who immediately made their escape on foot. The men ran down a nearby entry, followed by my father. He saw them enter an open door and followed them into the house. The men opened fire. My father returned the fire and three bullets hit the ringleader, Tom Williams. The others fired from the kitchen and my father was hit in the chest. He died immediately. The men retreated up the stairs before surrendering. Williams was treated at the Royal Victoria Hospital for his three wounds. After a lengthy murder trial, six men were sentenced to death for my father's murder. However, five of them had their death sentences removed and were given prison sentences.*

> *Williams was executed at Crumlin Road prison on the 2nd of September 1942. He was well-known to me, because we had sat together at the primary school. He was then a quiet young boy; he must have known my father, because he frequently called at the school.*

VE Day in May 1945 signalled the end of the war, at least in Europe. Celebrations were initiated across Northern Ireland.

> *The one thing I do remember was that there was an air raid shelter in front of our house, a red brick air raid shelter and at the end of the air raid shelters there used to be refuse bins, which were just like ordinary galvanised bins, which you put your potato skins and stuff in, and these were used to feed pigs which were used to feed people, which were part of the war effort. On this occasion somebody from somewhere had got a big ... I suppose it was one of those thunder flashes, and put it underneath one of these inverted bins. And I remember this bin rising about 20 feet in the air coming down with an unmerciful bang!*

Not all stations seemed to have received the memo that the war was over, however.

> *And we had heard nothing, bear in mind no television at that time, and very few people had radios, about what was happening in the big outside world. Was the war still on or just over in Europe? We did not know anything at all, until we heard that a very big bomb had been dropped in Japan. And the commandant decided that he would reinforce the fire-fighting team and we increased it by two men. And when we look back now with hindsight, and what we know of the atomic bomb, I don't think six men in Enniskillen would have been much effective against the bomb.*

Although the air raids had left one sergeant, six constables and two Specials dead, and two police stations destroyed, the RUC could boast of three policemen being awarded a George Medal and two other officers receiving British Empire Medals for bravery displayed during the German attacks.[12]

Chapter 7

Women in the RUC

The first women police in Northern Ireland in training in 1943. Standing (L-R) G Drennan, S Sherrard, F Brock, G McBrien. Seated: R Jones, Head Constable Major J Cherry, Woman Sergeant M Macmillan, M Bruce. This photograph was taken before the design of the very smart uniform and unique cap.

> *The Women Police Branch was a branch on its own at that time, just like the Detective Branch, it had its own hierarchy.*

> ∽

> *The two people on the panel were Sir Richard Pim and I had never seen such a handsome man before, he was really*

Women police at Brooklyn 1954. Main party Sir Richard Pimm, Judge Hanna, W/Head Constable Marion Macmillan.

> *lovely, and the other person was Woman Head Constable Macmillan. Now this was Marion Macmillan and she was the lady who started the women police in Northern Ireland she came over from the London Met in 1943 so that was my first vision of a woman – policewoman.*

Marion Macmillan

It is fair to say that without Marion Macmillan the introduction of female police officers into the RUC may have fared less successfully. Under her able stewardship, in April 1943 the first female recruits began their training programme.

> *We took whatever teaching they gave to the men there [the Depot]. But once we came out, she [Marion Macmillan] just finished the whole thing over. And she was a marvellous*

> *teacher, because she was in the Metropolitan. There was no such thing as saying, 'Oh my God! I'd better not ask her.' She was very pleasant and very, very good to us, and taught us well.*

The fondness with which Macmillan is remembered by female members of the RUC attests to the respect and authority which she earned during her time at the helm of the Women's Section. By the time she retired in 1965 her legacy was reflected in the growing range of tasks and jobs for which future women within the Force would be given responsibility and the high degree of professionalism with which they went about them.

> *She was a Scot and she started the Women's Police in 1943. In 1993 I brought out a book called 'The Women in Green' and that actually was a tribute to Miss Macmillan because I thought she did so much for us and only for her we would never have had these good jobs that we had and she left a great foundation for us to follow.*

> *I always thought that Miss Macmillan should have been granted some tribute when she left in '65, but there was nothing really, she just left the 'Evergreens' – it's a group of retired Policewomen and we meet every now and then.*

Early Duties

Initially, female members of the RUC undertook restricted duties with the emphasis placed on a limited range of policing tasks deemed unsuitable for male officers, particularly cases involving women and children.

Reviewing files, 1960s

> *Then there was a woman Head Constable, so we had our own hierarchy and we didn't do the same duties as the men; it was all to do with Welfare Police Duty, dealing with women and children and morals and that type of thing.*

> *We were mostly dealing with children right enough, mostly girls, but also women. And, we didn't go near the men, the men looked after themselves and we looked after our lot.*

Looking 'after our lot' often meant dealing with female prisoners, especially escorting girls to the Juvenile Court from the training homes or taking them to the homes after conviction.

There was also a particular public and promotional stress placed upon the duties that female officers were tasked with.

An arresting trio at Leopold Street, Belfast 1960s.

We were on foot patrol round the city and we were very elite in those days, we had to be all dressed the same and we carried brown gloves and we were much photographed in those days.

For some newer members of the force, however, such a prominent public role presented its own unique problems.

We were very conscious that we were actually representing the women police section of the RUC, so everything had to be done very, very well. If we saw an officer in the car, and because cars were so few all those years ago, we used to salute them. If the Lord Mayor came out of the City Hall in his car we had to go to the edges, salute him. If a funeral passed, we had to do exactly the same. And the first time we saw the Lord Mayor coming out of the City Hall in his car we got so flustered that we got into a telephone box in Donegall Place until he passed. Luckily nobody ever caught on.

Some of the other major duties for female members were far less glamorous.

We were in plain clothes and quite a lot of our duty was carrying out observations for indecent exposures or thefts or anything like that and of course there was always missing girls. At that time I think we must have known or at least knew every toilet in Belfast from the GNR to the one underground at the City Hall. We used to go round all these toilets at night looking for these missing girls and all the attendants in those toilets knew us and they would give us information.

The Impact of the 'Troubles'

With the onset of the modern 'Troubles' attitudes towards women police, both within and beyond the organisation, began to shift drastically.

Prior to the 1970s policewomen were only coming in every two years to fill the vacancies due to marriage. After 1970 they were coming in to fill vacancies because men were engaged with the 'Troubles' and women were being slotted into doing other duties and it was a gradual integration.

Women police were now not only engaged with a wider number of duties but were also integrated more fully with the rest of the

In Belfast wearing a high visibality coat, 1955.

Force. This development was partly due to the decentralising of the Women's Division in 1956. From then on women police officers served throughout the whole region – not just in Belfast – and in all the police divisions. In 1972 the Force was augmented by a Women's Reserve Force.

> *Another thing that came too was the Women Reserve. I had to do all the home visits and the home interviews so that was one of my duties at that stage.*

The 'Troubles' would also impact upon some of the more traditional areas of female police work as new security measures displaced previous patterns of criminal activity.

> *Our duties changed in Belfast city centre because we had a ring round the centre at that time and there were searchers. The prostitutes in the city centre found a change too 'cause they couldn't operate there. So a new thing that started was 'Massage Parlours' and these opened up in quiet residential areas.*

In the context of a deteriorating security situation, numerous female officers were injured and killed. These casualties had a disproportionate effect upon female members, because of their relatively limited number in relation to their male counterparts.

> *I have sad memories too about the RUC. While to me Newry was a happy place and I still have many friends and I go back there, it's sad that I knew each of these girls [who were killed] personally.*

Chapter 8

Sport in the RUC

Chaps who were good at sport were nearly always guaranteed to go up to Belfast; those who were good for nothing much usually ended up about the border, which is what happened to me.

'Sport Was Always Part of our Lives'

Sport within the RUC was used to help foster the necessary physical and fitness levels needed for members to fulfil their various daily duties. From the first day of training at the Depot a high premium was placed upon physical activity and sporting ability for new RUC recruits. As one former member remembers of his time at Enniskillen:

There was sport, bags of sport. If there was a game going on, football or tennis or cricket or football, you could count me in. I was in my element.

Another RUC officer recalled how sport 'was always part of our

CHAPTER 8: SPORT IN THE RUC

Traditional sport in the police – RUC Tug of War, 1923.

lives'. In fact, for some it was an interest in sport that determined their enlistment in the RUC.

> *There was a policeman called Denver Cardwell, who was a constable then, and Denver used to be from a part of the world called Derry Curry in Portadown, and we had a football team that I used to play for. So Denver had the bright idea that I should consider joining the RUC. And up until that moment in time I liked calling at the police station but I never considered joining them. So I thought of the football side and I made my application to join the RUC. I could kick a ball but I wasn't any good at the pen and I failed the entrance exam.*

Sporting Rivalries

Sport was also used to help cultivate a spirit of community within the force and there were some healthy rivalries between the various police divisions. They played against each other at rugby and football during the winter months and cricket in the summer. These sporting rivalries often extended beyond the RUC and, at times, across the border and into the Republic.

> *In those days [the late 1950s], it was possible to have home and away football matches with the local Guards. I particularly remember the days at Pettigoe where there was one police station on the northern side, and there was another one on the southern side, and the police force from the Irish Republic, and we arranged football matches together.*

Sport further helped connect the RUC with forces in the UK thereby helping to promote relationships at both an individual and group level, as well as providing a forum to showcase the skills of the men and women of the RUC across the water. Not surprisingly, given the prominence of firearms training, relative to other UK

J. Harkin joined in 1944 and joined the RUC Small Bore Rifle Team. He participated at Bisley for 32 successful years. He scored 100 points in ten matches in 1955/56

CHAPTER 8: Sport in the RUC

Ex Head Constable Hayes is seen refereeing a boxing match at the 1960 Rome Olympics.

divisions, the RUC proved to be a winning team at various shooting competitions.

> *The RUC Clay Pigeon Club was formed in 1972 and by '74 we were a very strong force and winning quite a lot of trophies across the water at the British Police Championships. In 1977 I won the British Police Championships outright and even today the RUC Clay Pigeon is still a strong force to be reckoned with.*

> ∽

> *I shot for the RUC in competitions across the water in the Police Championships. In fact we won the Championship nine years in a row!*

The RUC produced a range of sportsmen and women who became individual national and international champions in such different areas as golf, boxing, shooting, swimming and running. Many officials who contributed to the management of games came from the police family.

Sport also allowed the RUC a means to communicate more effectively with the various communities they policed, helping them to engage with locals in a way not possible when 'on the beat'.

> *I recall playing a friendly match at Grosvenor Park. There was a guy called Charlie Tully, who was a famous international player, and we used to play together in those days, and play friendly matches with people from that area [Springfield Road]. In fact, in the summertime of '67/68, you used to have summer leave in Belfast, and as a police force we used to be encouraged to try to community mix, realising that there was always a deep threat from the west Belfast Catholic republican area.*

In the wake of the violence in 1969, it was therefore not surprising that sport proved to be of particular value with the establishment of a more systematic RUC community relations programme.

Chapter 9

The Customs Unit

Border at Kileen showing Sgt Ed SMith RUC on right.

My task was Customs, specifically smuggling, and I certainly knew how to catch smugglers after being in South Armagh. I taught the men how to make cases, I taught them how to find illicit spirits called poitín, and we made many seizures of those, and every time there was a seizure of poitín, if they were involved, they got a money grant

85

> *as well as a favourable record. So, they enjoyed the work immensely in Derrylin when I was there, though times were quite hard.*

From 1 April 1923 trade across the land boundary between the Irish Free State and Northern Ireland became classified as foreign trade and a Customs land frontier was established to control land traffic. The Customs control was closed on Sundays and public holidays. Although the Customs Boundary Posts were staffed by Land Preventive Men, the duty of patrolling the roads for illegal imports/exports and for out-of-hours customs control was given to the RUC on behalf of HM Customs and Excise. The first patrols on the roads were carried out by the newly formed RUC and not the Customs Waterguard. This required the RUC officers to be commissioned by HM Commissioners to give them authority to administer Customs law. The Patrols, furthermore, were under the direct command of RUC District Inspectors and County Inspectors and they were also required to keep in touch with the local Customs Surveyor.[13]

Due to the fact that many of the Customs Posts were situated in remote rural locations, their condition was often very basic.

> *It was an awful station. It was a miserable place, nothing happened, we were near the border but nothing happened. There was no running water in the Post, there was no toilet facilities, a dry toilet outside somewhere. And there was a ghost – that sums it up. And, I was there for four months. But, I have to tell you that, if you wanted to wash there, you had to go to the shore, down to the, Lough Erne, take off your clothes, get your soap, wash yourself, go in and swim yourself clean, dry yourself and come back. That was a tough life.*

CHAPTER 9: THE CUSTOMS UNIT

"Ok, so I told you to wear civvies on Livestock – but my God man –". *Cartoon courtesy Police Service Gazette*

The task of the RUC customs patrols was to observe all persons, vehicles, livestock and merchandise crossing the Boundary in either direction by other than on the approved routes. In other words, a large part of the job was containing cross-border smuggling.

> There was a lot of smuggling going on both sides. Flour and stuff going out, hardware stuff, horse nails stuff like that, and coming in would have been liquor and eggs and butter ... An unusual thing about it was these ladies, women folk came in and when you brought them in they had these corsets on them lined with pockets for putting eggs in, the smell was terrible. That's what they had. Poor people!

> *Belleek was an interesting station on the border. Quite a bit of smuggling went on there and I remember one time we stopped some lorry carrying pigs and then we searched the house, the farmyard, and found pigs there. Some of them had been killed that day and others hadn't. The live pigs were seized by the livestock branch, and the Customs and Excise seized the dead ones.*

One former officer recalled what life was like on customs patrol.

> *Newtownbutler was known as a smuggling area for cattle, sheep, pigs. There's a lot of loughs, a lot of islands up round by Newtownbutler, Crom Castle. There was an RUC boat was allocated for us to do our boat patrols in among the islands, to do, watch out, look out for smugglers, or look out for poitín runners, people that maybe making their poitín.*

Some officers were seen to be engaging in somewhat dubious relationships with the local smugglers. A former Customs Officer recalls an officer returning home after a poker game in Newry.

> *He's going home on the bicycle after being in a poker game in the station and after losing all his money. He's going down along the road where he lived and the first thing the road's full of black cattle! So he stopped the bicycle and put his foot in the edge of the footpath and steadied himself, and sat there until they go past, and as they're going past a fella walks over to him and says 'There you are, all the best', put something into his hand and walked on. He never saw him before it and he never saw him after it. There was £100 in the envelope.*

By 1948 the RUC believed that Customs control was not a

constabulary function and detracted from detecting and preventing crime.

> But when Sir Richard Pim [Inspector General] took over the RUC his views that the Police shouldn't do Customs Duty – that was for civilians; police were crime. So he made a change there.

In 1951 the Waterguard took over the customs patrols and a Special Customs Unit was formed, which was staffed by ex-sergeants and higher grades from the RUC.

From the mid-1950s until the early-1960s Customs Posts became decidedly dangerous places. As mentioned in Chapter 3, the IRA's Border Campaign often included lightening strikes on isolated and vulnerable Customs Posts.

> Customs stations along the border were a favourite target for the IRA and were frequently attacked by gunfire and blown up. This meant that army personnel had to guard them to try to prevent further attacks. Killeen Customs post was one of many dotted along the border dividing North and South. It was situated six miles south of Newry, on the main Newry to Dundalk road and about 100 yards on the northern side of the border, leaving it vulnerable to attacks, especially from the southern side of the border.

> We done a lot of reconnaissance patrols round Customs huts, bridges, up round that area. Ambushes, those days Customs huts seemed to be the main targets.

The onerous task of protecting Customs Posts was certainly not a duty for the faint-hearted.

Sometimes we were given the responsibility of guarding the Mullens Customs Post, which of course was also situated on the border. A small village called Blacklion, which was in the South, was a short distance down the road. This was also a creepy and eerie place at the dead of night. There were cattle pens round the place providing your only form of shelter and protection. The Customs station was an old wooden hut, manned by one Customs man and was hardly worth protecting.

Unsurprisingly, patrolling the border could be a tense affair, the slightest nocturnal noise enough to set nerves jangling and gun triggers primed for release.

On one occasion while on ambush duty around a border customs post, it was in the middle of the night, I heard footsteps close-by. Taking precautions, I had a look round and found to my relief that it was a stray donkey. Let's say it was a very lucky animal that it was still alive because at that time security was so high that we thought it was very suspicious.

Chapter 10

Postscript – The 'Troubles'

The 'Troubles' changed everything; you didn't know where you were going or what you were doing at that time at all.

∽

The 'Troubles', all those years really, that I was in the police, from 1966 to 1968, you could say times were normal and there was no terrorist activity. So from '68 right until I retired, I policed in an environment of completely a terrorist environment at all times.

August 1969

The late 1960s was a period of massive change in Northern Irish politics as a civil rights movement emerged. The street politics used by the movement was played out against a backdrop of growing tension, as witnessed by the Divis Street riots of 1964 and the murder of three civilians by the newly formed loyalist paramilitary organisation the Ulster Volunteer Force in 1966. By the mid-1960s one policeman recalled how there was a growing realisation within the Force that 'this place [Northern Ireland] was about to boil over'.

During this period, the RUC found itself dealing with a large number of demonstrations and counter-demonstrations but without sufficient personnel or equipment to contain the situation.

> *During the first riot in Derry there were 72 policemen up. There were thousands of rioters, it was horrendous and they sent to Belfast for reinforcements and 12 men came, that made up the entire Reserve Force which was about 100 odd men. This went on for days and that's all there were and we took an awful pounding; and the water wagon – we ran out of water after the first 20 minutes but it was used as a sort of barrier that the boys could hide behind.*

> *And of course the 'Troubles' started in the late Sixties, so that made a lot of difference to the RUC: the uniforms changed and the kit changed. I remember doing riot duty down the Shankill Road, where you were wearing motorcycle, so-called crash helmets; but they weren't really safe things; and bin lids for shields.*

By the summer of 1969 the Force was over-stretched and over-burdened. Rioting in July and August in Belfast was contained, but only just. One officer recalls the marked change caused by the disturbances.

> *This was to be my first experience of the hatred and viciousness that mankind was capable of generating and it was physically directed towards the police. I was one of*

> *a number of policemen sent up to Belfast at that time to help to contain the situation and became involved in baton charges and fighting that followed.*

With the annual Apprentice Boys march in Derry fast approaching in August 1969, the RUC braced itself for further disturbances. At the conclusion of the parade serious violence broke out between protesting nationalist crowds and the RUC, a riot which was soon titled the 'Battle of the Bogside'.

> *Bad, bad riots, oh aye it was serious it was really bad, it erupted in Derry and I remember the Senior ACC saying to me: 'We're going to be driven back into Belfast …we do not have the resources to deal with this.'*

~

> *We were there for two days and I remember having to sleep in a shop doorway and it was late the next day before we were eventually pulled out, pretty tired and taken back to our home stations but certainly it was an awful experience that day.*

On 14 August 1969, exhausted and under intense pressure, the RUC withdrew from the Bogside and was replaced by soldiers from the Prince of Wales's Own Regiment. Instantly, the law and order situation in Northern Ireland was transformed and for the next thirty years policing would never be the same.

> *And the police were withdrawn from the Bogside and I amongst them. And I remember that withdrawal, up the hill, back to the Diamond. ... And it was a defeated people, you could see the dejection all round. And a colleague made the remark, he says, 'They're pulling us out. How*

will we ever go back and police that area again?' And that was very true. That really was the end of the police force carrying out normal police duties in an area where they weren't wanted. A significant change.

The Hunt Report

After the events in Derry, large-scale communal violence broke out in Belfast and between 14 and 16 August 1969 an estimated 1,820 households were displaced, nearly 300 homes burnt and seven people killed. In response to the destruction, an 'Advisory Committee on Police in Northern Ireland' was established, headed by Lord Hunt, to 'recommend as necessary what changes are required to provide for the efficient enforcement of law and order in Northern Ireland'.

" Well, sarge, I'm ready for those sweepin' changes they intend to make."

Cartoon courtesy Police Service Gazette

CHAPTER 10: Postscript – The 'Troubles'

> *In 1970 there had been a Hunt Report done on the RUC and various other reports followed it and it was decided that everything within the RUC was going to have to change. They changed the rank structure within the RUC. We no longer had an Inspector General, we had the Chief Constable, we had the English rank structure.*

The Committee put forward a series of recommendations, like relieving the RUC of all military duties, changing its ranking structure and disarming the force. These reforms found little support amongst most rank and file and the appointment of Sir Arthur Young, formerly of the City of London police, proved to be controversial.

> *The worst thing they ever did to my mind was to bring over officers from England in charge of the RUC. The first man we had here during the start of the 'Troubles', the first thing he did when he came over here, he objected to a police constable driving his car, to drive him around. And he promoted that man on the spot just by saying, 'You're promoted'. Because he wanted a sergeant to drive him.*

∽

> *The new I.G., or later to become the first Chief Constable, Sir Arthur Young, I don't think he really understood Northern Ireland.*

The changes proposed by the Hunt Report, particularly the disestablishment of the Ulster Special Constabulary, proved unpopular for many unionists. In the wake of its publication, protesting loyalist crowds clashed with the British Army on the Shankill and, on the night of 11 October 1969, during the disturbances, Constable Victor Arbuckle was shot dead. He was the first member of the RUC to be killed during the 'Troubles'.

> *Later in summer of 1969 the first RUC man to be murdered took place on the Shankill Road, and that was a constable called Victor Arbuckle, and I remember very clearly the night that he was shot dead by the loyalists on the Shankill Road. At the same time great unrest was erupting in the Ardoyne area of the district, and the situation deteriorated very rapidly, and life for a policeman in that area became very difficult.*

> *1969 also saw the Hunt Report, and that led to the RUC being disarmed, and although that only lasted a short time, because they were armed early in the 70s. And, because it was clear that the police could not continue to do their duty without being armed, because they were becoming the target for terrorism and were being attacked. And the first policeman I think was shot in 1969 in Shankill Road, a fellow called Arbuckle, in the Shankill Road, was the first policeman to be shot. And, so the police were rearmed again.*

The 'Troubles'

With the beginning of the 'Troubles' the men and women of the RUC faced a new reality which many had not anticipated when they had first joined.

> *I didn't like the terrorist stuff to be honest with you 'cause I didn't join the police to do that, I joined the police back in the sixties.*

For many their lives would never be the same again. Everyday

CHAPTER 10: POSTSCRIPT – THE 'TROUBLES'

tasks and routines were adapted and changed and even the most normal activities took on an abnormal air. Going for a game of squash could be fraught with danger.

> *We used assumed names and whatever the fictitious name was we would have entered on the booking sheets for booking squash courts. But even at that, we still went into the squash court with your towel and I always made a practice of keeping my revolver under the towel at the front of the squash courts. And indeed on one occasion an RUC member was shot at the Queen's University sports centre.*

Family life became strained as members of the RUC became targets when off-duty, leading to the imposition of extraordinary security measures at home.

> *We lived our lives constantly in danger and under threat from the IRA ... Our house felt like a virtual fortress. We had bullet proof glass in our windows, bullet and bomb-proof doors and infrared beams and floodlights to alert us if anyone was approaching our house. There were a number of panic buttons in our house which set off a siren and sent a radio signal to the local police station. ... This was a scary way to live.*

> *Personally, it was to change my family life, my personality and scar me mentally for the rest of my life. This was the beginning of what was commonly known as the 'Troubles', which was to last for the following thirty years.*

Members of the Force endured a terrible cost in the line of duty with a total of 302 RUC officers losing their lives and over 10,000 receiving injuries during the course of the 'Troubles'. Added to this was the unquantifiable mental and psychological burden with which many RUC members would have to live for the rest of their lives. Their gallantry and the resilience of their families were recognised in the award of the George Cross to the Force by H. M. The Queen on 23 November 1999.

Notes

[1] Chris Ryder (2000) *The RUC 1922-2000: A Force Under Fire*. London: Arrow, pp. 47, 48.

[2] Ibid. pp. 45.

[3] Graham Ellison and Jim Smyth (2000) *The Crowned Harp: Policing in Northern Ireland*. London: Pluto Press, pp. 66.

[4] Ryder, *The RUC 1922-2000*, pp. 90.

[5] To an unpublished thesis.

[6] Ryder, *The RUC 1922-2000*, pp. 80.

[7] Ibid. pp. 94.

[8] Lord Hunt Committee (1969) *Report of the Advisory Committee on Police in Northern Ireland*. Belfast: HMSO, Cmnd. 535.

[9] Bob Purdie (1990) *Politics in the Streets: The Origins of the Civil Rights Movement in Northern Ireland*. Belfast: The Blackstaff Press, pp. 30-31.

[10] BBC On-Line.

[11] *Belfast Newsletter*, 17 April 1941.

[12] Ryder, *The RUC 1922-2000*, pp. 75.

[13] Much of the background information on the Customs Unit comes from: Gilbert Denton and Tony Fahy (1993) *The Northern Ireland Land Boundary 1923-1992*. Belfast: HM Customs and Excise.

Interviewees Cited

Auld, Jim
Brown, Dessie
Brown, William
Burch, Kenneth
Cameron, Margaret
Cummings, Trevor
Dempsey, Frank
Dickson, Freddie
Dunleavy, Brian
Dyer, Martin
Faulkner, Myles
Finlay, Hugh
Forde, Ben
Greenway, Frederick
Glover, Wilbert
Halligan, Ernest
Heslip, Richard
Hogg, Douglas S.
Hutchinson, Francis A.
Kennedy, Frederick
Knowles, Gordon
McGimpsey, Ian
McGimpsey, Ross

McLaughlin, Emily
Millligan, Don
Moorehead, Basil G.
Montgomery, William
Mullan, John
Musselwhite, Maud
Penney, Ross
Ross, Herbie
Roycroft, Thomas
Russell, Thomas
Seaton, George
Selfridge, Joseph
Sinclair, Robin
Sinclair, Thomas G.
Sloan, Kenneth
Spiers, Alexander
Temple, James
Totten, Eric
Walker, Patricia
Walkingshaw, Terry
Wilson, Spiers
Wright, Richard

Our Volunteer Interviewers

Roy Black

Edna Caldwell

Stephen Corbett

Patricia Fawcett

David Hammerton

Maureen Hanvey

Valerie Harley

Jean Irvine

Roger Maxwell

Noel Moore

Ken McClean

Frances Orr

Joe Rawson